To the Shops

Written by
Stephen Rickard

Ransom

Jin is at the shops.
Jin has lots of bags.

3

Chun will go to the shops.
Chun will get a box of fish.

Will Chun go to
the shops on a yak?

Nen will go to the shops.
Nen will get a dish of nuts.

It is such a lot of nuts.

Nen can get a mug
of nuts as well.

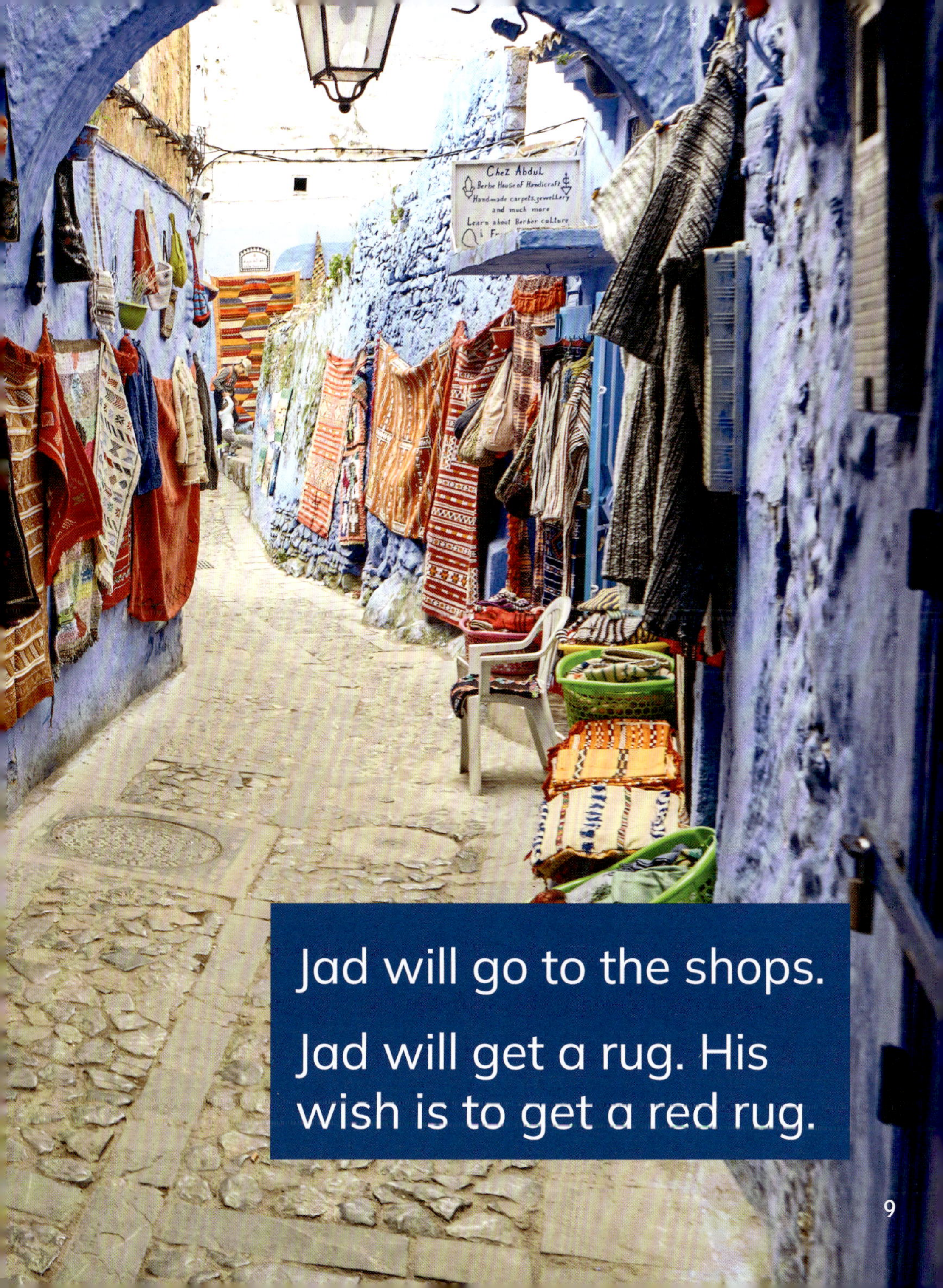

Jad will go to the shops.

Jad will get a rug. His wish is to get a red rug.

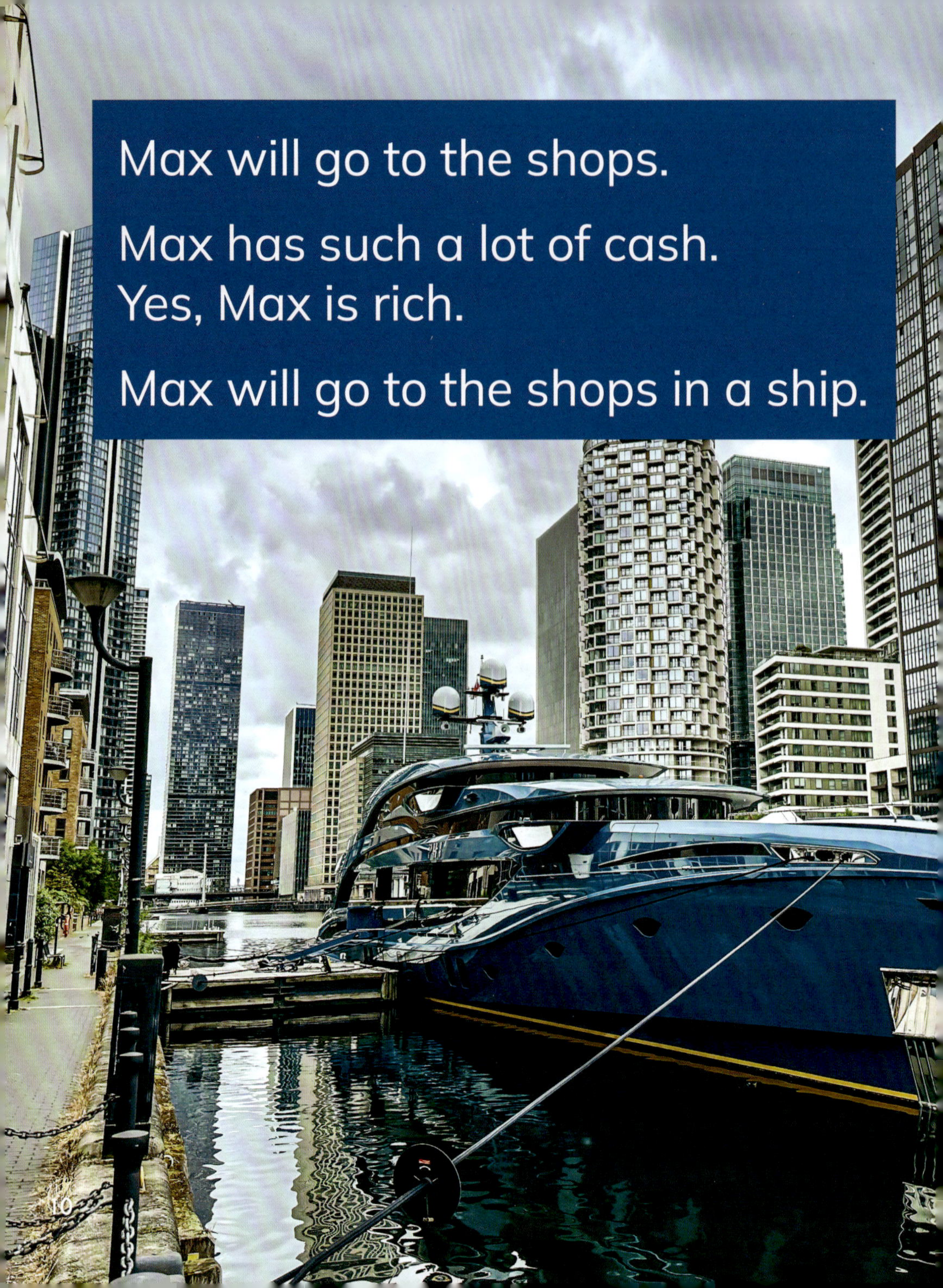
Max will go to the shops.

Max has such a lot of cash.
Yes, Max is rich.

Max will go to the shops in a ship.

At the shops Max will get a jet.

I will go to the shops.
I will get a jet as well.
But the jet I will get is
not as big.